NEVADA PUBLIC LIBRARY

T 43537

W9-CKI-328

JNF 796.8 CASEY
Casey, Kevin
Kung Fu

07/16

1/95

DATE DUE

NEVADA PUBLIC LIBRARY
631 K AVENUE
NEVADA, IOWA 50201

Illustrated History of
MARTIAL ARTS

KUNG FU

by Kevin K. Casey

illustrated by Jean Dixon

Nevada Public Library

THE ROURKE CORPORATION, INC.
VERO BEACH, FL 32964

ACKNOWLEDGMENTS

I am grateful to Diane Covalt and Robin Casey for the production and selection of the photographs for this book. I also thank two of my former teachers: Dr. Jerry Craven for introducing me to the world of writing, and Sensei Lee Gray for my introduction to martial arts.

PHOTO CREDITS

Photography by Diane Covalt

© 1994 The Rourke Corporation, Inc.

All rights reserved. No part of this book may be reproduced or utilized in any form or by any means, electronic or mechanical including photocopying, recording or by any information storage and retrieval system without permission in writing from the publisher.

Library of Congress Cataloging-in-Publication Data

Casey, Kevin, 1967-
    Kung fu / by Kevin Casey.
      p. cm. — (Illustrated history of martial arts)
    Includes index.
    ISBN 0-86593-368-5
    1. Kung fu—Juvenile literature. [1. Kung fu.] I. Title.
II. Series.
GV1114.7.C38 1994
796.8'159—dc20   94-4087
                                        CIP
                                        AC

PRINTED IN THE USA

TABLE OF CONTENTS

1

ORIGINS OF

K U N G F U

Kung fu is the name given to many of the martial arts of China. In Chinese, the words "kung fu" mean "task" or "hard work." The Chinese call martial arts *wu shu*, meaning "war arts." Most Western martial artists call kung fu "Chinese boxing."

There are many theories about the origins of kung fu. Some theories claim that kung fu began in China. Other theories state that it began in India, while yet others say that kung fu originated as far away as Greece.

Some theories promoting Chinese origins of kung fu claim that Chinese monks closely watched the way that animals fought each other. The monks would then imitate the fighting animals when practicing self-defense. This is why many kung fu techniques are named after animals.

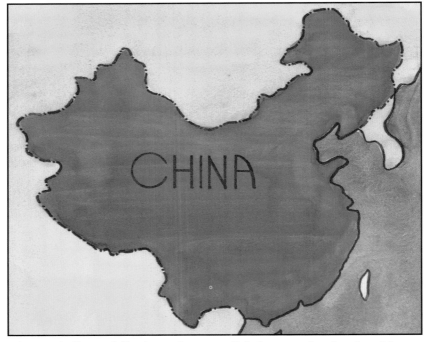

The words "kung fu" refer to the many fighting arts that developed in China. Some of these fighting arts have ancient origins. Others are less than 500 years old.

Some historians believe that kung fu evolved from the ancient Greek fighting art Pankration, which was brought to India by Alexander the Great's army in 334 B.C.

Another theory states that kung fu was based on a brutal type of fighting that began in Ancient Greece. In 334 B.C., Alexander the Great's army had conquered all of the land between Greece and the Indus River Valley in India. At that time, the Greek soldiers practiced a fighting style called Pankration. Pankration combined both boxing and wrestling. The people of India watched and learned Pankration, and eventually carried the fighting skill across the Himalayan Mountains into China.

2 BODHIDHARMA

Probably the most popular theory for the origin of Chinese kung fu is that it began in India about 1,400 years ago. According to legend, a rich prince in southern India gave up all of his possessions and began wandering throughout the countryside seeking the truth. The prince learned of the Buddhist religion and meditation.

Meditation is the practice of deep breathing exercises and concentration on only one thing. Another part of meditation is a series of physical exercises. Proper meditation takes much practice to master. One legend states that the prince became so good at meditation that he sat motionless for nine years, doing nothing but staring at a wall and listening to ants.

Eventually, the prince became a Buddhist monk, changed his name to Bodhidharma, and voyaged across the Himalayan Mountains into China. In his travels through China, Bodhidharma stopped at the Shaolin Monastery, far to the east in Northern China. Bodhidharma noticed that the monks were in poor physical condition. To improve their health, he taught them many meditation techniques.

Because of the meditation techniques, the monks' health soon improved. The grateful monks were eager to learn more about meditation from Bodhidharma. He taught them all he knew. The meditation techniques taught by Bodhidharma became a standard practice of the Shaolin monks. These techniques eventually evolved into kung fu.

The wandering Buddhist monk, Bodhidharma, taught the Shaolin monks exercises that later became a type of kung fu.

3

THE S H A O L I N

No other legendary figures in the history of kung fu are as well-known as the Shaolin monks. The Shaolin monks lived and practiced kung fu at the Shaolin Monastery in the Honan Province in Northern China.

The Shaolin monks continued to practice kung fu long after the death of Bodhidharma. Chinese legends are full of stories about the Shaolin monks as the greatest of fighting men, capable of almost magical powers. When the emperor needed help defeating an invading army, he sometimes called on the Shaolin monks. Even today, stories about the Shaolin monks are popular.

Shaolin monks practiced kung fu for many hours every day.

The Shaolin monks' mastery of kung fu made them the most formidable fighters in China.

The Shaolin monks did not make it easy to become a student of kung fu. First a potential student had to go to the Shaolin Temple and wait outside for many days, regardless of the weather. After waiting, a potential student might be let inside – only to be examined further. If, after much examination, a person was considered worthy of teaching, the physical and religious training could begin. A student was constantly evaluated by his instructors, and would only continue to be taught so long as the instructors believed him to be worthy.

4

The Shaolin monks believed their art was important and too dangerous to be taught to just anyone. They made it difficult for anyone to leave the monastery with knowledge of kung fu. When a student wanted to leave the monastery, he had to pass a test. It was believed that only the dedicated and trustworthy could pass the test.

First the student had to pass through a long corridor. The floor of the corridor was built with boards that were sensitive to footsteps. When the student stepped on the boards, he triggered dummies that swung clubs, swords and other weapons. The student had to defend himself against the dummies.

If the student managed to reach the end of the hall, the final and most difficult test remained. Blocking the exit was a heavy urn filled with hot coals. The student had to move the urn by grasping it with his forearms. A figure of a dragon was on one side of the urn. On the other side was a figure of a tiger.

When the student touched the sides of the urn, the forms of the dragon and tiger were branded onto his arms. After passing this test, the student was free to leave. The two brands were known and respected throughout China.

In order to pass the final test, a Shaolin monk had to lift a caldron filled with hot coals.

KNOWLEDGE

11

5

OTHER

S C H O O L S

INSECTS AND MONKEYS

The Shaolin were not the only Chinese to practice and teach kung fu. There were hundreds, maybe even thousands, of other schools. Many styles of kung fu were invented by people who closely observed the way that animals fight.

One style of kung fu is named after an insect, the praying mantis. The most famous technique in praying mantis style kung fu is "The Mantis Claw." Just like a praying mantis grabs another insect, a person skilled in praying mantis kung fu can grab an opponent and injure him.

Another type kung fu is called *ta sheng men*, or monkey boxing. The movements of someone performing monkey boxing look very much like the way a monkey moves about. The style was invented by a man who observed the sneaky way that monkeys fight. In monkey boxing there are many moves designed to trick an opponent.

The most popular form of kung fu practiced today is called *wing chun* style. Wing chun was invented by a Buddhist nun about 400 years ago. Wing chun style is considered to be the most lethal of all of the kung fu forms, and it is the only kung fu style that was invented by a woman.

The Praying Mantis stance is named after the praying mantis, an insect that looks something like a grasshopper.

6

THE SPREAD OF

K
U
N
G
F
U

FROM ASIA

The first time many non-Chinese were exposed to kung fu was in 1900. In that year, much of the land in China was held by foreign countries. Some of the Chinese people did not like their nation being run by foreigners, and they revolted. Many of the people who took part in the rebellion were skilled in kung fu. The foreigners who saw them fight noticed the rebels' skill and referred to them as boxers. The revolt was called the Boxer Rebellion.

Many of the Chinese who immigrated to the United States in the 19th century were skilled in kung fu. They started schools in some of the larger American cities, but few, if any, of the students were non-Chinese.

It was not until the 1960s that Western interest in kung fu increased. In that decade, a Chinese American named Bruce Lee began to make movies about kung fu. The audiences were thrilled with Bruce Lee's fighting and gymnastic ability.

Though the Bruce Lee movies generated interest in kung fu, many people criticized them. The critics claimed that movies about kung fu depicted martial arts as street fighting, and did nothing to show the true spirit of the arts.

The Chinese revolt of 1900 was named the Boxer Rebellion. The rebels who took part in the revolt were skilled in kung fu.

14

Some students of
kung fu still wear
traditional uniforms.
The uniforms are
usually black and
white. Colored sashes
are worn to
distinguish rank.

A kung fu school is called a *kwoon*. A kwoon can be any place that kung fu is taught, whether it be in a school building, a home or in a backyard. Teachers of kung fu are called *sifu* by their students. Beginning students learn from both the sifu and from more experienced students.

In many U.S. and European schools of kung fu, the students wear colored sashes around their waists to designate their rank and skill level. Many of the sash colors are bright. The highest grade of rank is generally designated by a black sash. In traditional Chinese schools of kung fu, sashes are not worn because rank is not considered important.

In all schools of kung fu, a student must always be respectful to his teacher and fellow students. This behavior is supposed to carry over into life outside of the kwoon. A student of kung fu should always be courteous to other people and never use kung fu for bad purposes. Outside the kwoon, the fighting applications of kung fu should only be used for self-defense. A student of kung fu must never fight if there is any other option.

THE K W O O N

Some students of kung fu practice with wooden devices. This wooden dummy spins each time the student strikes or blocks one of the wooden arms.

THE
MIND
AND THE
BODY

There are two general types of kung fu, the "internal" styles and the "external" styles. The internal styles emphasize mental energy, and they are mainly defensive. The external styles emphasize body strength, and they are more aggressive. Styles of both general types are still practiced today.

For self-defense, the internal styles of kung fu rely on redirecting the energy of the attacker. A person skilled in an internal style of kung fu always yields to an attack, rather than meeting it head-on. Those who practice the internal styles say that the energy of opponents can be redirected against themselves.

Internal styles teach that the real energy comes from the mind, not the body. People practicing internal styles often spend a lot of time in meditation. For this reason, internal styles, such as *tai chi*, are popular methods of physical fitness. Many elderly people in China practice tai chi well into their 70s and 80s.

Though mental energy is also important in external styles of kung fu, the majority of the techniques are physical blocks and strikes. In many external styles, wooden devices are used to toughen the arms and legs so that a more powerful block or strike can be delivered. In some schools, a student might practice by fighting a wooden dummy.

Meditation is an important part of kung fu. Meditation helps clear the mind and improve concentration during kung fu training.

The Crane
stance resembles
the bird that it is
named after.

9

In traditional types of kung fu, one of the very first things a student learns is how to stand properly. In order to execute any technique in kung fu, whether it be defensive or offensive, one must first be in the proper stance.

The horse stance is one of the first that a student of kung fu learns. The feet are farther than shoulder-width apart, with the upper portion of the legs parallel to the floor. The student's back must be kept straight. The arms are bent, with fists held against the body half way between the waist and armpit.

For a beginner, the horse stance is impossible to maintain for more than three minutes. Eventually, a student should be able to maintain the horse stance for several hours. The horse stance develops leg strength and balance, and improves posture.

Other stances are more directly related to self-defense. In wing chun style kung fu, students are taught to always stand with one side facing the opponent. This makes it more difficult for an opponent to strike the vulnerable spots located in the center of the student's body.

Standing with one side facing an opponent makes it more difficult for the opponent to strike vulnerable spots located in the center of the body.

10

DEFENSE:

B L O C K S

Along with knowing how to strike an opponent, a student of kung fu must know how to avoid being hit. This is often accomplished by blocking an opponent's strike. Students of kung fu spend as much time learning how to block as they spend learning how to strike.

One example of a kung fu block is the rising back-fist. If an attacker launches a punch to the face or head, the student of kung fu can block the punch by using the rising back-fist. As the punch is approaching, the student raises an arm with the hand open and intercepts the punch. Contact between the punch and the block occurs with the back of the student's hand and the underside portion of the attacker's wrist. If the rising back-fist block is executed properly, the punch will be deflected upward and the student will not be hit.

The rising back-fist block can be used to deflect a punch to the head.

The man in the white pants has used the heel of his palm to block a kick.

Almost every blocking technique in kung fu also involves preparation for a follow-up strike. This is because the attack may continue after the first strike is blocked. After students of kung fu become more advanced, they can execute blocking and striking techniques in combination.

11

FISTS, PALMS AND FINGERS:

HAND

TECHNIQUES

Part of self-defense involves knowing how to use offensive strikes to stop an attacker. When used properly, the hands are an effective weapon. Kung fu uses the hands in a greater variety of ways than any other form of self-defense. There are closed-fist strikes, as in boxing or *karate*. There are opened-handed strikes that involve the palm of the hand or use of the fingers. There are even ways to hold the hands that imitate animals.

One common hand strike is the palm-heel strike. This strike uses the bottom part of the palm. The fingers are held close together and slightly curled. The thumb is bent, with its tip pointing in toward the center of the palm. This strike is launched somewhat like a regular punch. The palm-heel strike is effective against targets like the attacker's jaw or nose.

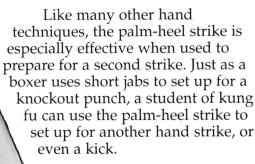

Like many other hand techniques, the palm-heel strike is especially effective when used to prepare for a second strike. Just as a boxer uses short jabs to set up for a knockout punch, a student of kung fu can use the palm-heel strike to set up for another hand strike, or even a kick.

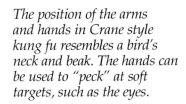

The position of the arms and hands in Crane style kung fu resembles a bird's neck and beak. The hands can be used to "peck" at soft targets, such as the eyes.

The man on the left has used his right arm to block a punch and deliver a palm-heel strike to the chin of his opponent.

12

LEG AND FOOT TECHNIQUES:

K I C K I N G

Proper use of the feet and legs are a valuable part of kung fu self-defense. Some styles of kung fu place much emphasis on kicking, while others have only a few kicks. Some of the styles of kung fu use high-level kicks that can hit an opponent in the chest or head. Other styles, such as wing chun, have only low-level kicks.

The crescent kick is found in several styles of kung fu. As the name implies, the crescent kick swings in circular motion. This kick is especially effective against an attacker's hands, and it can sometimes be used to knock a weapon out of the attacker's grasp. The crescent kick begins with both feet on the ground. From there, the knee is raised, as if executing a front kick. Instead of kicking straight and out, an inward circular motion is used. Impact occurs with the instep of the foot.

Some styles of kung fu use high and powerful kicks.

Being able to block and strike simultaneously is an important part of kung fu self-defense. The man on the left has blocked a punch and launched strikes to his opponent's throat and knee.

Like many other kung fu techniques, the crescent kick is useful in setting up a second strike. One common follow-up to the crescent kick is the spinning back-kick. This combination of kicks requires speed, balance and timing. It is one of the many combinations of techniques an advanced student of kung fu is able to execute.

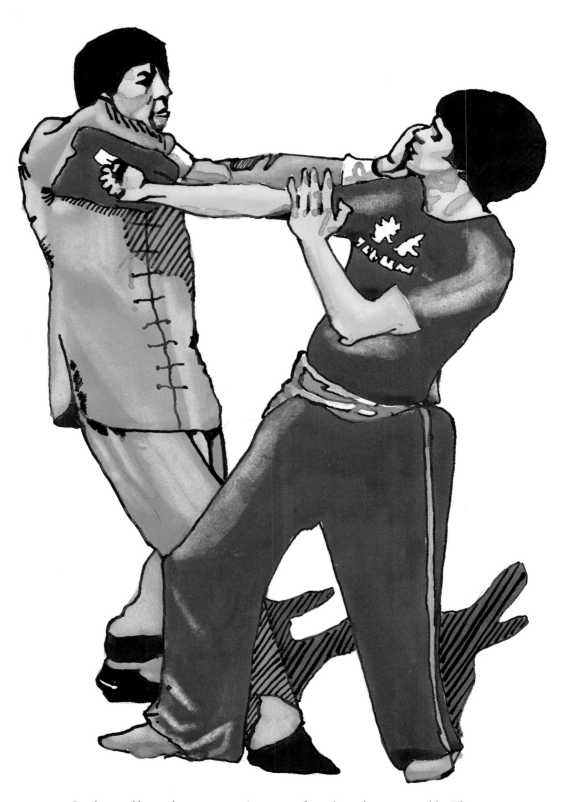

Students of kung fu must practice as much and as often as possible. These two students are practicing together.

13

Possibly the most lasting impact of kung fu is its influence on the history of other Asian martial arts. Okinawan karate and Korean *tae kwon do* were both influenced by techniques found in kung fu.

Okinawan karate became what it is today because of the combination of kung fu and Okinawan *te.* The founder of Goju-Ryu karate, Chojun Miyagi, traveled to China many times in order to learn kung fu. He combined the soft, yielding techniques of internal styles of kung fu with the hard strikes of Okinawan te.

Many Korean martial artists also traveled to China in the early 1900s to learn kung fu. When they returned, they combined what they had learned of kung fu with what they already knew of the Korean art of *soo bak.* The combination of the Chinese and Korean martial arts helped tae kwon do to become the popular competitive sport that it is today.

In kung fu's original homeland of China, interest in the art also increased in the 20th century. The Chinese still consider kung fu a valuable part of Chinese culture. The original Shaolin Temple is now a major tourist attraction.

The elbow can be an effective weapon.

THE LASTING INFLUENCE OF KUNG FU

14

KUNG FU

TODAY

Like many other martial arts, kung fu is practiced around the world. Though not as popular as other martial arts, such as karate or tae kwon do, kung fu schools can be found in many large cities throughout Asia, America and Europe.

Tai chi is an especially popular form of kung fu. In some large cities in the United States, tai chi classes are conducted during the lunch hour. These classes are a popular stress-relieving form of physical fitness.

With today's increasing interest in physical fitness and self-defense, the popularity of kung fu is expected to increase in the 21st century.

Knowledge of kung fu can be a valuable form of self-defense. The man on the right has used a crescent kick to knock a knife out of an attacker's hand.

Bodhidharma: a wandering Indian Buddhist monk; some theories about the origin of kung fu state that kung fu began with the meditation practices taught by Bodhidharma.

kwoon: a school of kung fu.

martial arts: any form of military training; often the term refers to empty-handed fighting, as well as to the various forms of exercises and sports developed from ancient fighting skills.

sifu: a teacher of kung fu.

soo bak: a Korean martial art; soo bak was combined with kung fu to produce the modern sport tae kwon do.

ta sheng men: monkey boxing; a form of kung fu that resembles the way that monkeys fight.

te: an Okinawan martial art; te was combined with kung fu to produce modern karate.

wu shu: the Chinese term for martial arts.

Tai chi is a popular form of physical fitness. People of all ages practice tai chi.

INDEX